VIRGINIA

Child Custody Guide

Determining the best interest for your child

Tatiana E. Mendez, Esq.

Jacobs & Whitehall
21750 Hardy Oak Blvd
Suite 104 – 51700
San Antonio, Texas 78258
(888) 570-7338
www.jacobsandwhitehall.com

Ordering Information:

Quantity sales. Special discounts are available on quantity purchases by corporations, associations, and others. For details, contact the publisher at the address above.

Orders by U.S. trade bookstores and wholesalers. Please contact Jacobs & Whitehall: Tel: (888) 991-2766 or visit www.jacobsandwhitehall.com.

Printed in the United States of America

Published in 2021

Dedication & Thanks

I'd like to dedicate this book to the amazing father of my own children, and handsome husband, Nick. Your unending support and belief in me has helped me to move mountains, and with you by my side I know that I can accomplish anything I put my mind to. Thank you for loving me as well as you do and for being a shining example of how to work together and compromise for happy children.

Thank you to my dearest friend, Bethany, for her expertise, friendship, and for always believing in me and seeing the best in me.

Thank you to Anna for helping me find my confidence when it was shot, and for always building me up and helping me to see myself through your eyes.

Thank you to Hannah for helping me keep my sanity in the middle of wild cases and for being my Kelly Clarkson song.

Thank you to Shelly, Liz, and Nick for being wonderful mentors and answering my endless barrage of questions, without complaint (most of the time).

Thank you to my son, Leo, for the happy family on the cover because custody cases are about children and their well-being, and everyone involved in custody cases can sometimes use a reminder.

Thank you in advance to my toddler, Matias, for not ripping the pages out of or eating this book.

DISCLAIMER

This publication is intended to be used for educational purposes only. No legal advice is being given, and no attorney-client relationship is intended to be created by reading this material. The author assumes no liability for any errors or omissions or for how this book or its contents are used or interpreted, or for any consequences resulting directly or indirectly from the use of this book. For legal or any other advice, please consult an experienced attorney or the appropriate expert, who is aware of the specific facts of your case and is knowledgeable in the law in your jurisdiction.

Tatiana E. Mendez, Esq.

505 S. Independence Blvd., Ste. 103
Virginia Beach, VA 23452
(757) 289-2499
www.virginiachildcustody.com

Testimonials

"Ms. Mendez is an amazing attorney she accepted my custody case with a truly open mind, given my nontraditional situation. She dedicated herself to my case giving me and my daughter great attention and care over a two- and half-year period. I'm a military member and was stationed over 2,000 miles from my daughter and a few times across the world. She worked hard to consult with me over a very difficult time and was able to attain for me a more than reasonable visitation schedule while on active duty and continued to work with me to gain a 50/50 order which my daughter and I are currently enjoying. Her knowledge and guidance of family law were invaluable to my family and me. I am truly thankful for all she has done."

– Matthew

****

"Easy to work with and no nonsense-Tatiana was great throughout the custody process and was easy to work with and her expertise of the law was fantastic. Hopefully, there is no need for her services in the future, but if needed I wouldn't hesitate to use her again."

– Sharona

****

"Tatiana was excellent. If I ever need a lawyer again I will use her services. I highly recommend her."

– Cynthia

****

"Exceptional! Mrs. Mendez was excellent when I approached her for my custody agreement! Listened intently and gave educated advice, I trust her and would definitely recommend!! The turnaround on the documents was fast as well!!"

– Amy

****

"Ms. Mendez helped me win primary physical custody of my son along with very favorable child support and an unintrusive visitation schedule. I was extremely impressed with her prompt responses to my questions and concerns, making me feel comfortable with the entire process. She did a phenomenal job negotiating in my best interests, especially considering how challenging and unreasonable my former spouse was acting. I would definitely recommend her to anyone, especially active duty military, looking for a fantastic custody/divorce lawyer!"

– Amanda

****

"She is OUTSTANDING!!! Tatiana is a wonderful, caring, passionate lawyer! If you need help with custody or divorce – look no further. She is GREAT in court! Very happy with how my case was handled."

– Anonymous

****

TABLE OF CONTENTS

About The Author

I have been a family law attorney for about seven years now, and in that time, I've successfully represented fathers, mothers, grandmothers, aunts, uncles, and cousins in all types of child custody and visitation matters. No two cases are ever the same, which makes this job extremely challenging but also very interesting. Often, my clients become like extended family members, especially in very emotional or difficult cases or in cases that go on for several months to several years.

For the parties involved, custody cases can be very overwhelming, so I try to give my clients a realistic analysis of their case and work with them to reach a sustainable outcome that's best for their children. These sorts of cases are important because they involve more than just knowledge of the law: a family law attorney needs to understand human nature, psychology, and negotiation. I've gotten into the habit of reading books on all three topics in my spare time. My undergrad focus was in psychology with a particular interest in social psychology and abnormal psychology; thanks to my career as a family law attorney, I get to use my undergraduate education in a way that I never would have anticipated.

What Do You Want Readers To Gain From Reading This Book?

This book is for anyone who may be going through a custody case in the Hampton Roads area of Virginia and is looking for some insider information and the general lay of the land. In my consultations with people who come into my office, I try to cover a lot of information, but obviously, it's not possible to cover *everything*. This book is my attempt to try to cover everything.

Custody cases are complicated and challenging. There are a lot of moving parts, people, and deadlines. This book is for all the parents and third parties who want to fight for what is in the best interests of their children but aren't sure where to start or what to do.

In my career, I've consulted with hundreds of people who have walked into my office scared and then left telling me that they feel better already. I want this book to be the paperback equivalent of a full-day consultation in my office in the hope that it helps people to better prepare for their cases and feel reassured walking into a courtroom.

CHAPTER 1

TYPES OF CUSTODY UNDER VIRGINIA LAW

The state of Virginia differentiates between legal and physical custody. The first type of custody available under Virginia law is legal custody, which can be sole or joint. Legal custody is the right to make decisions for your children regarding healthcare, education, and religious upbringing. In most cases, parents will have joint legal custody, which means that both parents have the right to make these major decisions for their children. If there is a disagreement, they have to discuss the issue with each other before making any major decision (e.g., deciding if little Hannah should have tubes put into her ears or whether little Mark should go to private school).

In some cases, one parent has sole legal custody. This means that only that parent has the right to make major decisions for the children and that parent does not have to consult with anyone else. While sole legal custody to one parent is rare, there are situations where it is appropriate, such as situations where the other parent is unable to make decisions for the children that are in the children's best interests or the parent is unavailable to make such decisions. This is true in instances where one parent is incarcerated or going through rehab for substance abuse or in instances of child abuse.

The second type of custody is physical custody, which determines where and with whom the children will live. Physical custody can be shared or split, or one parent can have primary physical custody. Shared custody is when both parents have the children for a significant amount of time per year, which means 91 days or more. As long as it works well for the children and is possible and reasonable, the ideal situation usually is for the parties to equally split their time with the children in a shared custody situation. Courts used to have a preference for mothers, which is an issue that parents bring up regularly in my consultations, but (luckily for good dads) that's no longer the case; in my experience, the preference has moved toward shared custody whenever possible.

Primary physical custody occurs when the children live with one parent most of the time. When we are talking about child support, you may notice a distinction between shared custody and sole custody. Sole physical custody is when the other parent has visitation with the children 90 days or less per year, which results in a different formula used to calculate child support than when the parties both have 91 days or more.

Split physical custody is unusual, but it does come up every now and then. Split physical custody involves multiple children with different schedules rather than the same schedule for each child. In general, judges don't like to split up siblings, but there are situations where it makes sense. I had one case involving four teenagers. The parents lived several hours apart, so it wasn't feasible to move the children back and forth very often. It was extremely overwhelming for one parent to have all four children at one time, and the children had different preferences regarding where they wanted to live. Those parents ended up each having two of the children during the school year and then alternated during the breaks with all four together so that the children could be reunited during holidays and summers.

The other aspect we talk about is visitation, or parenting time, which refers to the schedule that the parents follow. There are endless possibilities of parenting time schedules. You can find several examples of calendars online that show when each parent has the children. Parenting time can be as short as a few hours during the week to grab dinner with the kids or as long as a full summer, which is common in long-distance situations. There can be restrictions put into place regarding parenting time. For example, parenting time may be restricted to a particular location, city, or state, or may require supervision by an approved party or service.

CHAPTER 2

COMMON MISCONCEPTIONS ABOUT CUSTODY MATTERS

There are quite a few misconceptions that I hear regularly and I'd like to correct them with the truth.

Parenting time is treated separately from child support. Parents will often tell me that the opposing party is not paying child support so they should not see the child, or in the reverse, that the opposing party won't let them see the child so they don't think they should have to pay child support. This concept is sometimes called "Pay to Play," and the court is not impressed when parents come in on either side of this issue. Parenting time and child support are unrelated to one another. The court will not punish or reward a parent for their financial choices by using their children.

You cannot give up your parental rights without having someone take them over. Exasperated parents regularly ask how they can get the opposing party to sign over their rights to the child so that they don't have to deal with them anymore and can just collect child support. Uninterested parents ask me how they can sign over their rights so they don't have to pay child support anymore. It's easier to think of the concept of parental rights as parental obligations. The parents have the obligation to care for and support their children, while the children have the right to be cared for and supported. In order to sign over a parental obligation, there has to be someone willing to take over that obligation. The most common scenario where this occurs is a step-parent adoption. In these cases, the step-parent will take over the obligation from the biological parent, and then the step-parent is who is responsible for caring and supporting the child. The biological parent will have no more obligation, financial or otherwise, to the child, and therefore also will have no more say in what happens with the child.

The court does not favor mothers. It may have been the case in the past that mothers were favored over fathers by the court. I hear this all the time in consultations, in particular from fathers who had the court rule against them in a prior case. The court always decides custody cases based on what is in the child's best interest. Sometimes this favors the mother, but there are plenty of great dads out there with primary physical custody of their children as well, with the numbers increasing every year. Most judges now recognize that children benefit the most from a relationship with both parents, and the court usually tries to give children the benefit of both parents as much as possible. Sometimes a shared schedule is not feasible, but in my experience, that is the starting point for most judges.

Sole custody does not give you the right to shut out the other parent. Parents without sole custody still have certain rights. Regardless of which parent has custody, at a minimum, both parents still are entitled to access to the academic, health, and daycare records of their children. An exception to this is if access to the records would be reasonably likely to cause substantial harm to the child or someone else. If this is the case, the court's order will specifically state that a parent is denied access to the records.

CHAPTER 3

FACTORS DETERMINING BEST INTERESTS OF THE CHILD

Virginia courts decide custody and visitation cases by analyzing a list of factors that are supposed to help determine what is in the best interests of the child. This chapter will list each factor and then provide an explanation and analysis of what the factor means and what information or facts fall under it.

1. **The age and the current physical and mental condition of the child, giving due consideration to the child's changing developmental needs.**

This factor is solely about the child. The court wants to get an overall picture of the child and their needs and whether there is anything specific to this child that needs to be considered. This factor becomes particularly important if there are any special needs that require extra care, whether the care is from parents or professionals. This factor is also important regarding babies and toddlers because their developmental needs change very quickly, and a parenting plan designed around a newborn generally isn't going to work as well once the child begins attending school. Overall, these are the important questions to address: first, how is the child doing mentally and physically? Second, what care does this child need? And finally, what sort of care is the child going to need in the near future?

2. The age and physical and mental condition of each parent.

The court wants to get an overall idea of how each parent is doing physically and mentally to determine if there is anything that prevents them from being an appropriate parent. Generally, age and physical condition have a minimal effect on the court's opinion of someone's ability to parent unless either one of those presents a barrier for that person being able to effectively and safely parent. Great parents come in all shapes and sizes and ages, so most parents don't have to worry about a physical condition getting in the way of their custody or visitation.

A parent's mental condition is a very important aspect of the second factor. It can be tricky to bring in evidence of the other party's mental health because the court won't allow you to testify about your opinion (unless you're an expert witness). That means that even if you know for certain that the child's father is suffering from some mental health condition that renders him unable to be an effective parent, you can't simply say, "Your Honor, my son's dad is a narcissist and only cares about himself." You can only present evidence of events you personally witnessed and experienced and cannot offer diagnosis or an opinion. If there are real concerns regarding a parent's ability to parent due to their mental condition, the courts sometimes will require that parent (or both parents) to undergo a Parental Capacity Evaluation, which is an in depth evaluation by a professional, that involves various tests, interviews and other aspects. Parental Capacity Evaluations are generally expensive, and are reserved for complicated cases with serious concerns. Similarly, an expert witness can provide testimony regarding a parent's mental condition.

3. **The relationship that exists between each parent and each child, giving due consideration to the parent's positive involvement with the child's life and their ability to accurately assess and meet the emotional, intellectual, and physical needs of the child.**

This factor is an analysis of how the first two factors work together. Though it's not unusual for a child to be more attached to one parent over the other, it's very important to present evidence to the court that shows a positive and healthy relationship between parent and child. Being the less-favored parent doesn't necessarily mean you're going to lose your case, but you do want to show that you have a positive relationship that can grow moving forward. The key here is to demonstrate that you understand what the needs of the child are. I had a case once where the opposing party, the child's father, wanted to have primary physical custody of a toddler that he had never spent more than one hour with. It became clear in his testimony that he had no idea what the child's needs were. He could not explain what a full day with the child looked like, nor did he have a plan for child care for when he was at work. He also did not see any issue with immediately taking the child from the mother for a few weeks, despite the child barely knowing who the father was. Needless to say, he was not successful in his petition.

4. The needs of the child, giving due consideration to other important relationships of the child, including but not limited to siblings, peers, and extended family members.

With this factor, the court begins to look at other important people in the child's life, which becomes particularly important if the child has siblings at one house but not at the other, or if one parent is trying to relocate and wants to take the child with them. It's crucial to show the court that the child will be able to maintain and maximize the relationships they have built with important people around them with that parent's proposed plan.

It's not unusual to have military parents who are only in Virginia because of a military assignment. These parents generally don't intend to stay in Virginia because they don't have ties to the area aside from the military. If a parent is proposing relocating with the child, then extended family members living wherever that parent is trying to relocate can be important in persuading the court that the best interests of the child would be met elsewhere. It's salient to show the court evidence of who are the important people in the child's life. These relationships don't necessarily have to be present relationships; they can be potential relationships that the child doesn't have the opportunity to have unless the child is able to relocate or is able to live under the parenting plan that is being proposed by that parent. Important relationships to a child are not only family, but can also include others such as neighbors, friends, members of their sports teams, counselors or doctors.

5. The role that each parent has played and will play in the future in the upbringing and care of the child.

This factor looks backward in time to see how each parent has fit into the child's life so far. Generally, the courts value stability for the child, which means the court is reluctant to switch custody from one parent to another unless there is strong evidence to support that the switch would be in the child's best interests. For this reason, if one parent has been the primary caregiver of the child up to this point, it's most likely that parent will have an advantage over the other parent. This factor benefits the stay-at-home parent over the working parent who was not around much due to regular travelling for work, deployments, or the like.

It can be difficult for the working parent to overcome this factor when compared to the stay-at-home parent. Nevertheless, it's important to show the court that you intend to be as involved as possible moving forward, even if that wasn't the case in the past, as well as the reason *why* you weren't as involved in the past (i.e., military). Of particular importance for this factor is your involvement in things related to the child, such as doctor's appointments, school meetings, extra-curricular activities, etc. Don't forget the day-to-day tasks either, such as packing healthy lunches, helping with homework, tossing the ball in the yard and bed time routines.

6. The propensity of each parent to actively support the child's contact and relationship with the other parent, including whether a parent has unreasonably denied access to or visitation with the child.

This factor often makes or breaks a case. I've had cases where both parents were great parents but the court switched custody from the mom to the dad because the mom wasn't co-parenting effectively with the dad. Unfortunately, it's not unusual to have one parent calling the shots while the other parent tries to get whatever parenting time they can with the restrictions imposed by the first parent. Virginia courts believe that children need and benefit from having both of their parents. With that said, it's important to show the court that you can effectively co-parent, meaning you are able to work with the other parent to meet the best interests of the child and you're not unreasonably denying access to or visitation with the child or putting up unnecessary barriers for the other parent. Sometimes parents get comfortable in the roles they have settled into during the relationship, and do not do anything to change their roles after the relationship is over. This often results in one parent being the one who calls the shots with the child, while the other parent is simply along for the ride.

An issue that sometimes comes up with this factor is when the other parent asks the parent with the child to drop everything and allow them visitation. In other words, they will give the parent with the child one hour's notice or one day's notice and say, "I would like to have this weekend with little Meghan"; then, the parent with the child says, "Well, I already had plans for little Meghan this weekend, so that's not going to work." The next thing you know, the first parent is presenting these text messages in court and complaining about not getting visitation, when the request wasn't reasonable in the first place. This factor can be tough to navigate. The key here is whether the parents are being reasonable in working with each other and supporting the relationship between the other parent and the child. In a situation where one parent is being unreasonable, the best course of action is to respond with an alternative that is actually reasonable. "I already made plans and unfortunately am not able to reschedule, but would you like to have little Meghan next weekend beginning Friday after school? In the future, if you can give me more than an hour's notice, I would love to work with you to schedule more time."

7. **The relative willingness and demonstrative ability of each parent to maintain a close and continuing relationship with the child and the ability of each parent to cooperate and resolve disputes regarding matters affecting the child**.

The first part of this factor relates closely to the third factor, regarding the relationship between each parent and the child. The second part of this factor focuses primarily on each parent's ability to co-parent, and as such, is related to the sixth factor. Effective communication is pivotal here. The parties need to use positive language in speaking with each other rather than abusive and harmful communication. Text messages and emails are read in court all the time, and any threats made by one parent against the other parent, derogatory language or generally rude communication will not be viewed favorably by the court.

Additionally, neither parent should be using the children against the other parent or presenting any impossible scenarios. I had a case where one parent insisted that she had offered plenty of extra time to the other parents and that it wasn't her fault he refused it since he didn't care about his child. A closer look revealed that she only offered extra time during hours where he was required to be at work and would have needed to get special permission to take off the time to take her up on her offer. I have also seen a lot of cases where one parent tells the other that they can only see the child if they do something in return. Children are not prizes!

Each parent should be reasonable and willing to discuss issues and compromise. I have had countless cases where one party was fond of telling the other to direct all communication to their attorney. Unless there is something preventing an effective discussion between the parties, such as a protective order, parents should do their best to work together to compromise and find solutions. As the great Ruth Bader Ginsburg would say, "You can disagree without being disagreeable."

8. The reasonable preference of the child, if the court deems the child to be of a reasonable, intelligent, understanding age with the experience to express that preference.

This factor is generally relevant in older children. While there is no set age, the court typically considers children around age 12 to be able to articulate a preference in a mature and reasonable way. That doesn't mean that the child gets to decide where they live, and that's true for every age. As a child gets older and more mature, their preference does hold more weight, but the court will still balance all of the other factors to determine what is in the child's best interests.

In most cases, I don't like to have children testify. The court assigns a guardian *ad litem* to make a recommendation to the court regarding the child's best interests and their preferences. If necessary, I find that the best way to ensure the child's voice is heard in court is to have the child go back to the judge's chambers with the guardian *ad litem* and privately tell the judge whatever it is that needs to be said. You can read more about the guardian *ad litem* in Chapter 4.

9. **Any history of family abuse, which is defined as any act involving violence, force, and threat, including but not limited to any forceful detention that results in bodily injury or that places one in reasonable apprehension of bodily injury, and that is committed by a person against family or household members. If the court finds such a history, the court may disregard factor 6.**

While typically no factor is more important than any other, this one can definitely tip the scales heavily in favor of one parent over another. The propensity to support the child's relationship with the other parent is completely disregarded in abuse cases.

Abuse cases are extremely complicated, and unfortunately, it is tough to prove that abuse has taken place at all, which can make victims feel hopeless. The court system is generally reactive rather than proactive, which can make abuse cases additionally stressful. Navigating an abuse case is not something that any parent should attempt to do alone as these cases can be difficult even for seasoned family law attorneys.

10. Such other matters as the court deems necessary and proper to the determination.

This factor is a catch-all since it takes into consideration anything else that might be relevant.

The idea behind the ten factors is that the court wants to have a full picture of the parent, the child, and the circumstances in their lives. The court analyzes and weighs all of the factors—not necessarily equally—to make a determination on what will constitute the best interests of the child.

CHAPTER 4

GUARDIAN AD LITEM APPOINTED IN FAMILY COURT

A guardian *ad litem* (GAL) in Virginia is an attorney appointed by the court to represent the best interests of the children. Overall, GAL is responsible for conducting an independent investigation into the facts of the case, meeting with the children, and being an active participant in the custody and visitation proceedings. The first duty a GAL has is to establish a relationship with the child. GALs are required to meet face-to-face with the child and determine what the child's wishes are, along with the safety and adequacy of the child's current placement. The GAL decides if there is any need for further testing or evaluation or if the court needs to temporarily intervene with a temporary order or something else while the trial is pending.

The GAL's interactions with the child must take into consideration the child's age and maturity level, as well as the circumstances surrounding a specific case. The GAL generally will do a home visit at each home and speak to the parties and to other important people in the child's life in order to get a big picture of what the child's life looks like and how the child is doing. It's not uncommon for them to speak to neighbors, friends, or extended family members, as well as counselors, teachers, and anyone else the child regularly interacts with.

In court, the GAL's recommendation can hold a lot of weight, which makes sense considering the background work the GAL is supposed to do before making a recommendation. For that reason, I usually recommend that my clients treat the GAL like gold.

This person can make or break a case, and it's necessary to treat them with respect and avoid doing anything to create a negative opinion of you.

It's important to keep the factors regarding the best interest of the child in mind during any interaction with the GAL because that's precisely what their recommendation will consist of. Some GAL reports will list the factors outright and then put each relevant fact under the qualifying factor. A common mistake that people make is attempting to cast the other party in a negative light to the GAL. Don't forget, one of the factors is each party's willingness and ability to co-parent and resolve disputes with the other parent. You don't have to like the other parent, but your feelings about them are completely irrelevant. What really matters are the facts and how you're living your day-to-day life dealing with this other person.

I am a certified GAL, and I've found in my experience that the way that parties speak about the other party can be very telling. During one of my home visits in one particular case, I was sitting in the father's living room when he started to go down a laundry list of things he did not like about the child's mother. The kid was sitting right there on the couch between her father and the grandmother playing a videogame. It was the grandma who got up and removed the child from the room, saying, "I don't think it is appropriate for her to be listening." I don't remember specifically what the father said about the mother in that situation anymore, but the fact that he was so comfortable making disparaging remarks about the mother right there in front of the child said a lot. It was something I mentioned in my report to the court.

It's a better use of your time with the GAL to tell them all of the amazing things about your own parenting and how well the child is doing under your care or because of your interactions with them. It's perfectly fine to express concerns about the other parent, but it's crucial to make sure the concerns are based in fact and definitely to avoid expressing those concerns within earshot of the child.

CHAPTER 5

CUSTODY MATTERS IN JUVENILE DOMESTIC RELATIONS COURT VS. CIRCUIT COURT

Child custody matters usually start in the Juvenile and Domestic Relations District Court, or the J&DR court. The great thing about the J&DR court is the judges there spend a good amount of their time hearing all manner of custody and visitation matters; those judges have seen it all and have a great handle on the relevant law and all of the factors related to your case.

Circuit court judges hear a wider variety of cases, including appeals from the J&DR court, appeals from the General District Court, divorces, personal injury cases, wrongful death cases, serious criminal cases and most civil cases with claims of more than $25,000. If your child custody matter is related to a divorce, then the case will be in the circuit court along with the rest of the divorce. If it's possible for you to separate the other divorce issues from the custody issues, generally meaning that the other issues in the divorce are not as pressing as matters related to the children, then I generally recommend that people handle their custody matters in the J&DR court when possible.

In the J&DR court, you will automatically get a guardian *ad litem* assigned to your case. In the circuit court, you have to make a motion for the court to assign a guardian *ad litem*, and the payment to the guardian *ad litem* is mostly paid up front by the parties.

If you have a custody trial in the J&DR court and it doesn't go the way that you want, you can appeal it within a specified amount of time, and the appeal will then be heard in the circuit court. Appeals are heard *de novo,* which means they are heard as though they have never been heard before; therefore, anything that happened in the J&DR court didn't happen at all. You get another bite at the apple without the prior trial having an effect on it.

What Factors Lead A Custody Matter To Go To Trial?

Custody matters are some of the most emotional and challenging cases for parties involved. After all, children are often the most valuable and treasured part of a parent's life.

The first step to figuring out a custody arrangement is to discuss it with the other parent, if possible. If you can talk about what you want to happen in terms of a parenting plan with the other parent, this is the best way to figure everything out. Once you've got an arrangement made up, you can put it on paper, and then file it with the court to become a court order.

Of course, this isn't always possible. If you can't reach an agreement with the other parent, then the next step would be to file for custody and visitation with the court and have the court try to figure out what should be put into an arrangement to encompass the best interests of the child.

Once the petitions for custody and visitation have been filed, the first time you go to court is called an initial appearance. The initial appearance is not your full trial. At this initial appearance, the court will assign a guardian *ad litem*, an attorney assigned to the case to investigate and figure out what they believe is in the best interests of the children. They will make that recommendation later at the actual trial. At the initial appearance, the court will assign a trial date for a date and time in the future. At that trial, any issues that have not been settled will be litigated for the judge to determine what they think is in the child's best interests.

It's not uncommon for the parents to reach a settlement agreement in the days leading up to their trial date. There is a lot of negotiation and discovery during that time that can push parents toward coming to an agreement that is best for their child. Sometimes parents are able to reach an agreement on some issues and not all of them, in which case only the unsettled issues would be litigated. I have had several cases where the parents co-parented fairly well but then disagreed on a parenting decision, such as what school the child should attend. The trial was only about the one issue.

CHAPTER 6

FORMAT OF A FAMILY COURT TRIAL INVOLVING CUSTODY MATTERS

The purpose of a trial is for the judge to listen to both sides and examine the evidence to determine what is in the best interest of the child. There is a general timeline of events that occurs in trials. First, each attorney begins the case with an opening statement. This is each side's opportunity to tell the judge what the case is about and provide a general outline of what that side expects their evidence to prove in order for the court to rule in their favor. Once each side has given a brief introduction to their version of the story, then they each will present their evidence. Evidence is presented in the form of witness testimony and also exhibits, which can be documents, photographs, videos or other tangible items.

The petitioner in the case, which is the party that filed the case, goes first and calls their witnesses. After each witness, the opposing side, which is called the respondent, also gets the opportunity to question the petitioner's witnesses. The guardian *ad litem* and the judge will also be able to ask their own questions of any witness that is called.

The petitioner will ask each of their witnesses open-ended questions designed to elicit that witness's story or observation. This is called direct examination. Once the petitioner finishes questioning the witness, the respondent may ask the witness leading questions related to only the direct examination. Leading questions generally can only be responded to with a yes or a no. This style of questions is called the cross-examination. Most people have seen this portion of a trial on television and are likely familiar with cross-examination questions, such as "Isn't it true that you didn't pick up the child from school?" Once the petitioner has called all of their witnesses, the process repeats with the respondent calling their own witnesses and the petitioner cross-examining them.

When the respondent rests (meaning they're finished putting on their evidence), the petitioner may put on rebuttal evidence, which is evidence that contradicts or explains the evidence presented by the respondent. Likewise, the respondent has the opportunity to put on rebuttal evidence to contradict or explain the petitioner's rebuttal evidence, so it's a back-and-forth process for quite a while.

After all of the evidence has been presented, each side may give a closing argument. In their closing argument, an attorney summarizes all of the evidence that was just presented and wraps it up in a beautiful bow that highlights all of the best parts and makes the argument for their position to persuade the court. The petitioner goes first, then the respondent, and then the petitioner gets an opportunity to get the last word in and to briefly respond to the respondent's closing argument. Usually the guardian *ad litem* will give a closing argument as well, which often includes what their recommendation is for what is in the best interest of the child.

Usually, the judge will make a decision on the case immediately after each side finishes their closing arguments. Sometimes judges will take a brief recess to review the evidence or case law presented and then will decide the case. In more complicated cases or after a very lengthy trial, a judge may issue a written decision and provide it to the parties at a later date.

Once the final court order is entered with the judge's decision, the parties must immediately begin following it. If either party is unhappy with the outcome and would like to appeal, they have 10 days to do so after the final order is entered in the juvenile and domestic relations district court.

CHAPTER 7

EVIDENCE USED IN A CUSTODY CASE

The rules of evidence are incredibly complicated and complex and require thorough understanding before going into a custody trial. I've seen attorneys sink or swim when it comes to evidence, and even judges have gotten the rules wrong.

There are two main types of evidence: testimony and exhibits. Testimony is spoken evidence from witnesses. Exhibits can be almost anything—

documents, photographs, videos, records, emails, text messages, or even objects. Getting the judge in your case to listen to or look at, and then consider your evidence is one of the trickiest parts of a trial. You can use almost anything as evidence as long as it is relevant and does not violate the rules of evidence.

What Is Hearsay?

The biggest pitfall that people fall into is not being able to get their evidence considered by the judge because they do not correctly follow the rules of evidence. The most common objection is in regard to hearsay evidence. Hearsay is an out-of-court statement offered to prove the truth of the matter asserted. Hearsay can be spoken, like a remark made by someone, or written, like in a letter from a teacher. The logic behind not allowing out-of-court statements is that the person who made it is not present to be cross-examined. For example, if your child told you they prefer to live with you, you cannot use that statement to prove that your child prefers to live with you. The child's statement would be hearsay because it was made outside of court and you are trying to use it to prove the statement (that they prefer to live with you). If you wanted to get this evidence in, either the child would have to testify in court (or you would have to get the child to tell the guardian *ad litem*, who could then consider the statement when they make their recommendation). If you bring the person who made the statement in to testify, then they can be cross-examined and hearsay is no longer an issue. There are various exceptions to the hearsay rule, but understanding the basic gist of the rule is a good start.

Both testimony and exhibits can be excluded from evidence if either one is considered hearsay. In order to admit a document into evidence, a document needs to be properly authenticated. For example, if you want to submit a letter from your child's teacher, you need your child's teacher to be present to state that they are the one who wrote the letter and it has not been altered in any way. Without the teacher present, the contents of the letter are not admissible evidence to prove anything alleged in the letter, because it would be an out-of-court statement offered for its truth.

If you wanted to submit that same letter for a different reason other than for its truth, then it would be admissible. For example, if the teacher sent a letter home that said something like, "I think that little James has the flu as he was not acting like his usual self." The mother then picked up the child from school and took him to the doctor. She wants to introduce the letter as evidence to prove why she took the child to the doctor. The letter could be used to explain the decision she made, but could not be used as proof of James having had the flu. The decision the mother made is separate from the substance of the letter, so she could introduce the letter in court by saying, "This is what I received that caused me to make the choice I made," or, "This is what I received that gave me that opinion, regardless of whether that opinion was correct." In this case, the letter would be admissible because it's not being offered for its truth.

In other words, it does not matter whether James actually had the flu because the reason that statement is being offered as evidence is to explain why the mother took him to the doctor, not to prove that he was sick. As you can see, it's a very tricky rule, and I have seen attorneys (and even judges!) get it wrong time and time again. The key is that it is hearsay if the statement was made out of court, by someone who is not available in court to testify, and is now offered for its truth.

Witnesses

There are two types of witnesses: lay witnesses and expert witnesses. Most witnesses in any custody case will be lay witnesses, but it's not unheard of to have several types of expert witnesses in more complicated cases. The main difference between them is that lay witnesses can testify only to relevant facts and observations they have firsthand knowledge of, while experts can give their opinions on matters within their expertise. Generally, lay witnesses cannot give their opinion, and no witnesses can testify as to a conclusion of law. A witness can be qualified as an expert by knowledge, skill, education, experience, or training in the specialized field.

How Far Back In Time Can Evidence Go?

Another important consideration to know regarding evidence is that, in general, you can only present evidence of events or information that happened after the entry of the last court order. That means that if parties were divorced five years ago and have been following the custody and visitation schedule in their final decree, then they can only use evidence that happened after the divorce was finalized if either party petitions to change the schedule. The logic behind this requirement is that anything that occurred before the current court order was already considered when that order was decided, so there's no reason to re-litigate things. In most cases, only allowing new information to be considered does not present a problem; it streamlines the process and makes it easier to keep track of what is and is not relevant.

Sometimes, however, it can complicate cases, especially if there's something that occurred prior to the last court order that hasn't occurred since then but should still be considered. If there has never been a court order, then evidence can go as far back in time as you want, but it still must be relevant. If someone was convicted of a DUI, for example, it would make a difference whether the incident occurred last weekend or 10 years before the children were born.

Overall, it is tricky to navigate the rules of evidence and to figure out how to get all of the information in. That's really where a great family law attorney comes into play.

What Evidence Do I Need For Custody Case?

Judges decide child custody cases by trying to determine what is in the best interest of the child. When I begin a custody or visitation case, I often will print out a list of the Best Interest of the Child Factors for my client, so that they keep them in mind when issues occur and can figure out whether the evidence they have is likely to be helpful. A timeline of the facts and incidents that have happened is a good place to start. Keep a calendar showing when each party has the children and notate any significant events on it, such as if a party did not show up for a child exchange, or missed a parent/teacher conference. I tell my clients to document everything, but to make sure it is done in a cohesive manner that can easily be understood by an outside person. There is often an incredibly massive amount of evidence in custody cases, and organization will go a long way.

Really, any evidence that helps to explain your facts and supports your position is helpful. The reality is that you know your story better than anyone else; you are living it! Tell your attorney your story and then back up each part with evidence, which can be anything including photographs, videos, medical records, school records, and text messages, and phone records.

Do not neglect your witnesses! Ask anyone that you'd like to testify in court in your trial whether they would be willing to help you in your case. It's better to have people present who want to be there to help you, rather than witnesses who were subpoenaed to be there 10 days before trial and would rather not be involved in the first place. Speak to the children's teachers and doctors and find out what the opposing party's involvement is with them as well.

Consider what the opposing side is likely to say about you and prepare to handle that as well.

Look at the social media of the people involved. Take screenshots. Assume that the opposing party is doing the same and act accordingly.

CHAPTER 8

UNIQUE CASES

Relocation Cases

The Hampton Roads area of Virginia is home to a lot of military parents, which inevitably means that parents are forced to relocate due to their careers. This often results in the relocating party wanting to take the children to the new location, and the non-relocating party wanting the children to stay here. When there is already a court order regarding custody in place, relocation cases are unique because there are additional factors involved that the relocating party has the burden to prove.

The analysis the court considers has the following parts:

1. The petitioner must prove that there has been a material change in circumstances since the last court order.

2. If there has been a material change, the court must determine whether relocation would independently benefit the child and not just the parent. The factors in Chapter 3 regarding the best interest of the child are relevant here.

3. The court must determine whether the relocation will substantially impair the relationship between the non-relocating party and the child. This is also related to the best interests of the child.

When there is not a court order in place to begin with, the analysis is the same as any other custody case, which means the determination must be based on the child's best interest. Unless there are facts in your case to prove otherwise, it is in the best interest of children that they be able to spend time with both parents on a regular basis. Relocation cases are notoriously difficult to win for the party that is relocating because the standard is very high. If a parent is relocating for the military, then it is difficult to argue that the relocation would independently benefit the child. A connection to the place of relocation is something that could constitute an independent benefit to the child, such as extended family members or a school with a special program that the child does not have access to locally. Economic stability for the relocating parent has been considered by the court to independently benefit the child as well.

In cases where the non-relocating party is very involved with the child, winning a relocation case is almost impossible. This is because it is almost certain that relocation would substantially impair a relationship between the child and an involved parent, unless the distance allowed for the same level of contact between the non-relocating parent and child to remain. In cases where the non-relocating parent is not very involved, relocating parents stand a better chance of being successful in having the court grant the relocation.

There is a decent amount of Virginia case law on relocation cases with different scenarios where the court rules for and against relocation depending on the facts. If you have a relocation case, these cases are a good place to start to see where the facts of your situation fall compared to cases the court has decided in the past.

Third-Party Rights

Virginia law has what is called the "Parental Presumption" which means that the law favors the biological parents over third parties in custody and visitation cases. However, as you now know, custody and visitation cases are always decided based on what is in the best interest of the child. A third party with a legitimate interest may be awarded custody or visitation if they can prove it would be in the best interest of the child. Third parties with a legitimate interest can include grandparents, stepparents, aunts, uncles, and other relatives. The court has different standards depending on what the third party is asking for.

Third-Party Visitation

If the parents both object to giving a third party visitation, then the third party has to prove that the child would suffer actual harm to their health or welfare without the visitation. The most common third-party visitation scenario that I have seen is where grandparents want to have regular contact with their grandchild. If Meemaw can prove that little Cindy would suffer actual harm to her health or welfare then she may be successful, but this is a high standard that is extremely difficult to meet without expert witness testimony. If grandparents just want regular contact with their grandchildren because they think it would be nice, they would do best to save their time and money and play nice with the parents rather than trying to get a court order for visitation

If only one parent objects to the third party's visitation, then the court does not have to follow the standard requiring actual harm. Instead, the third party must show that the best interest of the child would be served by granting visitation to the third party.

Third-Party Custody

In a custody case between a parent and a third party, the third-party first has to overcome the parental presumption favoring the biological parent. There are a handful of factors that will overcome the parental presumption if proven, which include: (1) parental unfitness; (2) a previous court order giving the third party custody; (3) the parent voluntarily giving up the child; (4) the parent abandoning the child; and 5) special facts and circumstances. This is a completely different standard than third-party visitation.

I have had quite a few third-party cases. One of my clients was the child's aunt and she overcame the parental presumption by proving that the parents were unfit due to drug addiction. I had another case where my client was the child's grandfather and he overcame the parental presumption by proving that one parent had abandoned the child and the other parent was physically and mentally abusive to the child.

Once the third party overcomes the parental presumption, then the case proceeds as it usually would between two parents on equal ground, which means that the court considers the best interest of the child factors. The parental presumption only has to be overcome once, so if the case goes back to court at a later date, the standard is still what is in the best interest of the child.

CHAPTER 9

CAN WE APPEAL A FINAL CUSTODY ORDER?

In Virginia, both parties have an absolute right to appeal any final order of a judge in the Juvenile and Domestic Relations Court (J&DR). The appealing party has to note their appeal within 10 days from entry of the final order. A new trial will be scheduled in the Circuit Court for the case to be tried again. This is called a *de novo* appeal, which means the case starts over again from the beginning, without consideration for any rulings, evidentiary decisions, or anything else that happened in the trial in the J&DR.

While the appeal is pending, the order entered in J&DR remains in effect until the circuit court case is finalized. The parties still have to abide by the order from J&DR until the circuit court orders otherwise.

What Factors Must Be Present For Modification To A Custody/Visitation Arrangement?

If it has been over 10 days since the J&DR order was entered, you are no longer able to appeal the order, but may still be able to modify it with a motion to amend in J&DR. In order to modify your custody or visitation agreement in Virginia, you have to prove, first, that there's been a material change in circumstances since the last final order was entered and, second, that a change would be in the best interest of the children.

What qualifies as a material change in circumstances depends on the specific facts of any given case. Some examples of possible changes would be a parent has relocated, a parent has remarried or had another child, a parent has repeatedly and unreasonably withheld visitation from the other parent, or the child's needs have changed. You could, for example, have an order that was entered when the child was a newborn and breastfeeding and attached to one parent for many months; then, that child starts daycare or school and the schedule no longer makes sense for the child or for the parents. Depending on the facts of the case, the same incident may or may not constitute a material change. For example, if a parent relocates but it doesn't have an effect on the current parenting time schedule, then the parent's relocation may not be a material change at all.

The court will consider whether there is a material change in circumstances that warrants changing the order, and then if the court has determined that there is, the next step is to determine whether modifying the order would be in the child's best interest, which involves the factors that we discussed previously in Chapter 2.

Another way to modify an order is through an agreement between the parties. If all parties agree, then there's no need for a trial and no need to prove material change or that the change is in the child's best interest. The parties can simply ask the court to enter the new order with their agreed changes.

CHAPTER 10

TIPS FOR CUSTODY CASES

These are some general tips for being successful with your custody case.

1. **Pretend you are a contestant on a reality show.** When someone is on a reality show, everything they say and do is recorded and then put together later in whatever way the producers want to make that person appear like a villain or a hero. Assume everything is eventually going to be seen or read by a

judge, and act accordingly! Messages may be taken out of context, but if you maintain your demeanor at all times, then it will be harder for the opposing party to make you look like a villain.

2. **Document everything.** Keep a calendar and write down everything that happens. If there are issues with the opposing party not showing up for visitations or consistently being very late, then document the dates and times. Communicate via text or email whenever possible to keep a written log of communications. Take photos and videos.

3. **Be involved with everything related to the kids.** Go to all doctor appointments. Check-in with their teachers. Attend baseball practices and games. This will help you in your case but it also will make you a better parent if you weren't already doing these things.

4. **Be 100% honest with your lawyer.** If there are some bad facts in your case and I know them, then I can prepare for how best to handle them

in court later on. If I don't know about the bad facts until we are in the middle of a trial, then I am stuck at the moment without the same resources I would've had if I had been given the opportunity to think it through beforehand.

5. **Always follow your court order.** There are ways to deal with emergency issues that do not involve violating a court order. Talk to your attorney!

6. **Be a good human.** No matter who you are dealing with, whether it is the opposing party, guardian *ad litem*, opposing counsel, or your own attorney, treat them well. Be kind, polite, and reasonable.

7. **Dress for the position you want.** If you want the court to believe that you are a responsible, stable, and amazing dad, then don't show up to court wearing an offensive t-shirt or flip-flops. I ask my clients to play into stereotypes and dress like a mom or dress like a dad. It may not be super modern of me, but we have to use the cards we have, and the reality is that

psychological biases exist, and if we can use them to our advantage, we should!

8. **Make all decisions with consideration for the best interest of the child.** Look at the factors in Chapter 3, and act accordingly. I tell my clients that if they are unsure about what the right choice is, that they should see how they can justify their choices under the factors. If they cannot, then it's a poor choice.

9. **Call me!** I am here to help. I know how stressful a custody case can be, and I highly recommend that you do not go into one without a competent lawyer by your side. Your children are priceless and custody orders are hard to change, so you should definitely do everything in your power to make sure that your case is handled well.

INDEX

NOTES

Made in United States
North Haven, CT
05 August 2026

15984897R10044